SEASONS

Fall

by Mari Schuh

Kaleidoscope
Minneapolis, MN

Where the Quest for Discovery Begins

This edition first published in 2024 by Kaleidoscope Publishing, Inc.

Kaleidoscope Publishing, Inc.
6012 Blue Circle Drive
Minnetonka, MN 55343

Library of Congress Control Number
2023936902

ISBN
978-1-64519-717-1 (library bound)
978-1-64519-765-2 (ebook)

Bigfoot Jr. lurks within one of the images in this book. It's up to you to find him!

Table of Contents

Fall Is Here!

The bright Sun shines on a fall day. “Today is a great day to play basketball,” Tom says.

“Yes, the air feels cool and fresh. I love it!” Jen says.

FUN FACT
Fall is also called autumn.

The weather is cooler in fall. The **temperature** slowly drops. The air can feel chilly.

Fall weather can be rainy. It can be warm and sunny too.

Earth's seasons are spring, summer, fall, and winter. Fall comes after summer.

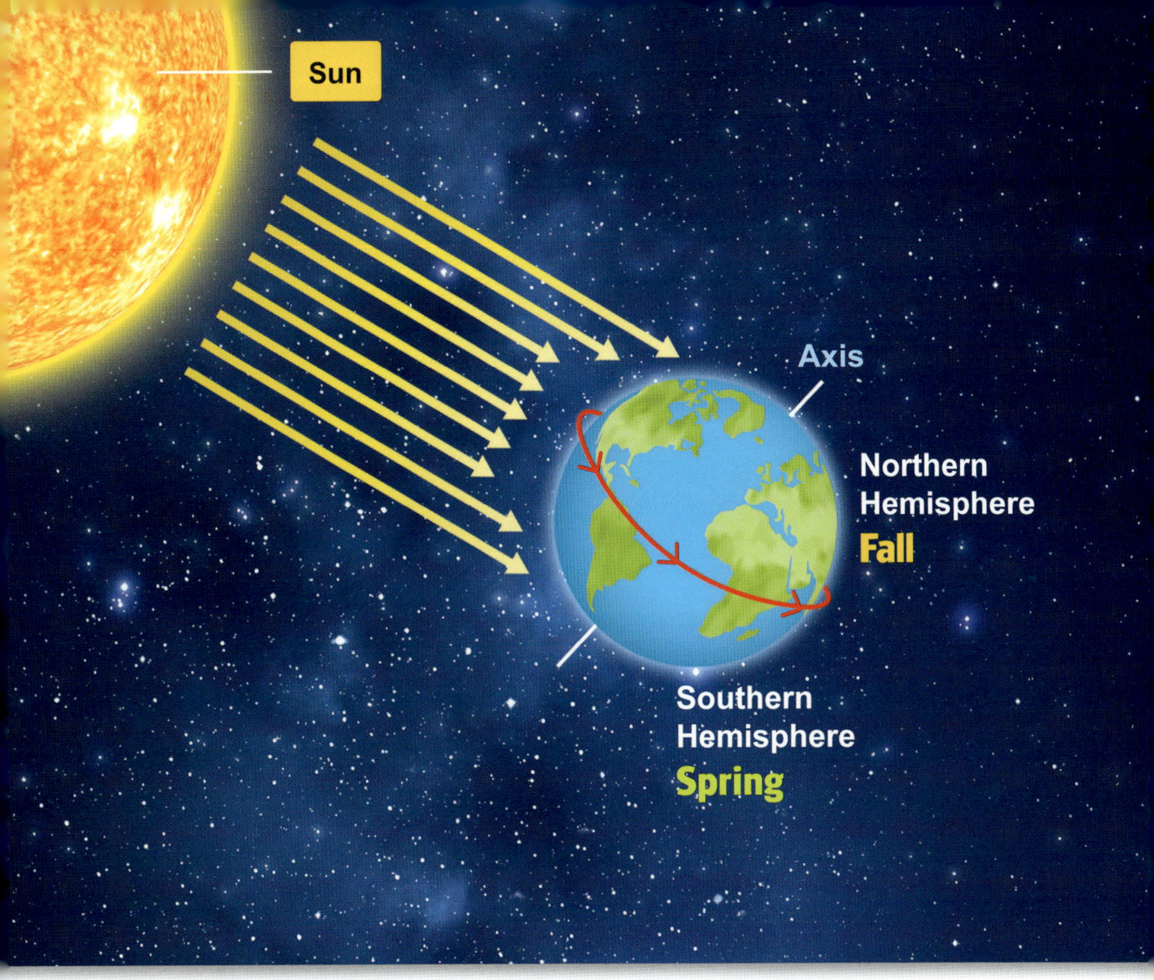

Earth **tilts** as it spins on its **axis**. As Earth travels around the Sun, some areas get more sunlight. Fall has less sunlight than summer. On Earth's northern half, fall starts in September.

Trees in Fall

Leaves turn colors in fall. They turn red, orange, and yellow. They turn purple too.

Leaves drop to the ground. They pile up. They blow in the wind. Soon the trees will be bare.

FUN FACT

Some people believe it is good luck to catch a falling leaf!

Fall Is Fun!

FUN FACT
Pumpkins grow from flowers.

People spend time outside in fall. They look at colorful trees and plants.

A new school year starts every fall.

FUN FACT
There are more than 7,500 kinds of apples.

People pick apples from trees. They pick pumpkins off vines. These **crops** are ripe in fall.

Farmers harvest crops in fall.

Leaves are dry and crunchy in fall. People rake them into piles. Then kids jump in the big piles.

What Do People **Use in Fall?**

What do you use in fall?

Animals Get Ready

In fall, animals get ready for the cold winter. Many birds **migrate**. They fly south to warmer weather.

Butterflies can migrate too. Before winter, many monarchs fly south. Millions of them make the long trip!

Monarch butterflies migrate about 3,000 miles (4,800 km)!

Ladybugs also eat more food in fall. They eat lots of small insects before the cold winter.

There is less food in winter. Raccoons eat more food in fall.

Squirrels are busy in fall. They bury nuts and seeds in the ground. They will eat them in winter.

“Jen, look at the squirrel! It found some food,” Tom says.

“It’s getting ready for winter. Winter will be here soon. Until then, we can look at all the fall colors!” Jen says.

Photo Glossary

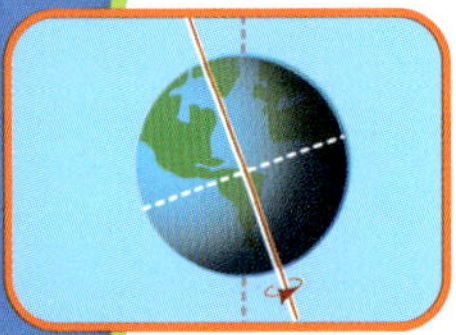

axis: An imaginary line through the center of Earth. Earth spins on its axis. One spin is one day.

crops: Plants grown for food. Corn, wheat, and beans are crops.

harvest: To gather crops. Farmers harvest many crops in fall.

migrate: To move to another area at a particular time of year. Some animals migrate to warmer areas every fall.

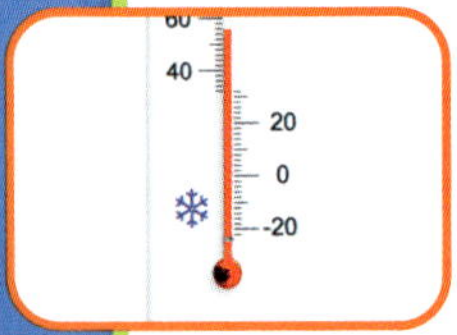

temperature: The measure of how hot or cold something is. A thermometer measures temperature.

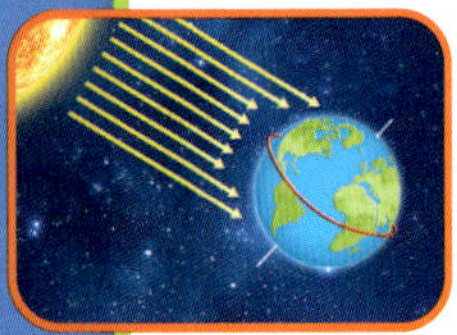

tilts: Leans, tips, or slants to one side. Earth tilts on its axis.

Read More

Earley, Christina. *In the Fall.* New York, NY: Crabtree Publishing, 2023.

Leaf, Christina. *Fall.* Minneapolis, MN: Bellwether Media, 2023.

Peters, Katie. *What Animals Do in Fall*. Minneapolis, MN: Lerner Publications, 2024.

Youssef, Jagger. *Seasons*. New York, NY: PowerKids Press, 2023.

Websites

FACTSURFER

Factsurfer.com gives you a safe, fun way to find more information.

1. Go to www.factsurfer.com.
2. Enter "Fall" into the search box and click 🔍
3. Select your book cover to see a list of related websites.

About the Author

Mari Schuh's love of reading began with cereal boxes at the kitchen table. Today she is the author of hundreds of nonfiction books for beginning readers. Mari lives in the Midwest with her husband and their sassy house rabbit. Learn more about her at marischuh.com.

INDEX

PHOTO CREDITS

The images in this book are reproduced through the courtesy of: Jan Pelcman/Shutterstock Images, cover (top left); diamant24/Shutterstock Images, cover (top right); photka/Shutterstock Images, cover (bottom); topseller/Shutterstock Images, title page; LilKar/Shutterstock Images, p. 3; Africa Studio/Shutterstock Images, p. 4–5; Sergey Novikov/Shutterstock Images, p. 6 (top); Tomas Ragina/Shutterstock Images, p. 6 (bottom); ju_see/Shutterstock Images, p. 7 (top); sun ok/Shutterstock Images, p. 7 (bottom); Mihai_Andritoiu/Shutterstock Images, p. 8 (all four seasons); sun ok/Shutterstock Images, p. 8 (circle); Madlen/Shutterstock Images, p. 10 (leaves); Joe Arrigo/Shutterstock Images, p. 11; Loren L. Masseth/Shutterstock Images, p. 12 (top); Michael O'Keene/Shutterstock Images, p. 12 (bus); GSDesign/Shutterstock Images, p. 13 (apples); smereka/Shutterstock Images, p. 13 (bottom); B Calkins/Shutterstock Images, p. 14 (top); LilKar/Shutterstock Images, p. 14 (bottom); My Good Images/Shutterstock Images, p. 15 (yellow boots); Iuliia Syrotina/Shutterstock Images, p. 15 (hoodie and stocking cap); Yellowj/Shutterstock Images, p. 15 (Halloween pumpkin); Lightspring/Shutterstock Images, p. 15 (basketball); VINCENT GIORDANO PHOTO/Shutterstock Images, p. 15 (mittens); Hurst Photo/Shutterstock Images, p. 15 (rake); Mtsaride/Shutterstock Images, p. 15 (football); photodaria/Shutterstock Images, p. 15 (vest and hooded sweatshirt); siraphat/Shutterstock Images, p. 15 (wheelbarrow); RG-vc/Shutterstock Images, p. 15 (checked blanket); Annette Shaff/Shutterstock Images, p. 16–17; Butterfly Hunter/Shutterstock Images, p. 17; PictureDesignSwiss/Shutterstock Images, p. 18 (top); Sonsedska Yuliia/Shutterstock Images, p. 18 (raccoon); George3973/Shutterstock Images, p. 19 (acorns); SarahLou Photography/Shutterstock Images, p. 19 (red squirrel); Africa Studio/Shutterstock Images, p. 20; Jan Pelcman/Shutterstock Images, p. 21; Tomas Ragina/Shutterstock Images, p. 22 (temperature); Annette Shaff/Shutterstock Images, p. 22 (migrate); smereka/Shutterstock Images, p. 22 (harvest); Alchemist from India/Shutterstock Images, p. 22 (crops); Tatyana Mi/Shutterstock Images, p. 23.